Radha

Leena Saldanha

Virgin
Leaf
Books

ISBN 978-93-52017-51-5
Copyright © Leena Saldanha 2016

First published in India 2016 by Virgin Leaf Books
An imprint of Leadstart Publishing Pvt Ltd

Sales Office:
Unit No. 25-26, Building No. A/1,
Near Wadala RTO,
Wadala (East), Mumbai – 400037, India
Phone: +91 96 99933000
Email: info@leadstartcorp.com
www.leadstartcorp.com

US Office:
Axis Corp, 7845 E, Oakbrook Circle,
Madison, WI 53717, USA

Disclaimer: The Views expressed in this book are those of the Author and do not pertain to be held by the Publisher.

Editor - Tanzeel Saiyed
Cover - Girish Rapatwar
Layout - Chandravadan R. Shiroorkar

Typeset in Palatino Linotype
Printed at Repro knowledgecast Limited, Thane

Dedication

To Krishna.
I wonder who you are today...

About the Author

Leena Saldanha is a writer, reader, cook, cat lover and food freak, besides being an inveterate procrastinator. Although technically she holds a graduate degree in Philosophy and a post-graduate one in English Literature, she has never allowed, to paraphrase Mark Twain, her schooling to interfere with her education.

She has worked with NGOs in the tribal hinterlands of Maharashtra, she has worked with the urban poor in the slums of Pune. And for the past decade and a half, has worked steadfastly towards a nervous breakdown caused by too much coffee and too little sleep in the mad, bad, ad world. In the ten years that she worked in one of Pune's biggest ad agencies, she spent 4 years as the agency's Creative Director and Chief Strategy Officer.

She went on to set up The Red Tree Design Studio, one of Pune's leading brand and business strategy consultancies.

Today, she runs The Red Tree, dotes on her two children, gets pampered by her dog and her parents, pampers her cat, and, along with her husband, dreams up new ways of making life interesting.

ACKNOWLEDGEMENTS

It takes a special kind of madness to sit staring at a laptop screen and type in surreal separation from what passes for the real world. And it takes an extraordinary kind of family to not merely accept but positively nurture such madness.

Thank you, Mom and Dad, for raising me to grow up believing that anything is possible. Thank you, Siddhant and Sanaah for loving a Mom who was often staring into space instead of doing something constructive like baking you cookies. Some Moms cook, some Moms chauffeur, some Moms write, but all Moms love. Thank you for understanding that at such a young age. Thank you to my many mentors who taught me some of the toughest lessons in my life.

Leadstart Publishing, you have been everything a new author could have asked for. Tanzeel, my editor, thank you for handling Radha with such love.

And finally, thank you, Abhijit. You are the answer to a prayer I didn't know I was praying.

CONTENTS

1.

There are wars
That you must fight
But the true warrior
Fights
With peace in her heart
For she has heard
Krishna speak
And unlike Arjuna
She has listened.

2.

You will chain me
To a desk?
Strap me to a
Deadline?

There is not one cell
That is dead inside me
I am awake
Alive

There is lightning in my heart
In my feet

And my jet black eyes
Glitter
With a light that shines from
Inside

This is when I feel most
Powerful
When someone tries to
Tie me down

This is when I throw my head back
And laugh

This is when I fly

You know that don't you,
Krishna

Which is why you invented
Deadlines...

3.

Some days my eyes hurt
With the weight of all the tears
I refuse to shed.
You can give me those tears,
Krishna
But you can't make me
Give them up.
And just fyi
They invented kajal
And lipstick
And I'm going out dancing.

4.

I stood under
The tree
Whose name I don't know

I'm not very good
With tree names
God knows why
I'm expected to be

But I stood under
That unlabelled
Tree

And a treacherous
Deceitful
Breeze
Brushed past me
Caressed my cheek

Teased a tendril
Out of my tightly coiled
Hair
And went his merry way.

He was the beginning
Of summer
In the middle of winter
Just ever so slightly warm
When I thought he would be
Cold

He reminded me of you,
Krishna

But then
What doesn't...

5.

There was a time
When I hadn't met you,
Krishna.

But there was never a time
I didn't know you…

6.

The air is cool
On my fair skin
This morning.

A little sharp
Like the bite
Of fresh lettuce.

There's a crunch
To the air
A punch
To the morning

Almost as if
Exactly as if
You are smiling
That charismatic
Smile of yours

The one you smile
When you are up to
Something.

What are you up to
Now,
Krishna...

The day is feeling
Deliciously
Mischievous

On my
Fair
Skin.

7.

I can't not speak to you
For prolonged periods
Of time.

I feel like I'm running out
Of oxygen
Like my life force
Is ebbing.

I feel like the earth
Must be feeling
When she breaks up
Into dull lifeless clods
In the absence
Of the benediction
Of rain.

I feel like the drunkard
Must be feeling...
Tortured
Desperate
In the absence
Of the mercy
Of poison.

My need of you
Is like that,
Krishna...

Elemental.
Agricultural.
Dangerous.

8.

Today I wake
With a heavy heart.
A feeling of dread
Has settled somewhere
In my stomach.

Millenia have passed
Since I was a village belle
Krishna

Today I have mountains to climb.

Mountains with weird names
Like
How-do-I-manage-this-client
And
Can't-they-see-I'm-doing-my-best
And
Too-much-work-too-little-sense.

You lifted the Govardhan
I remember.

I couldn't ask you to leave
Other pressing matters
And rush here
To lift my mountains
Or anything

But you think you could lend me
Your little finger,
Krishna

So what if I'm not
Draupadi.

9.

Speaking of Draupadi
You say you were her
Friend...

Shouldn't you have
Had a word
With dear Yudhishtir
After you'd finished
Covering her up?

She became the victim
Dushyasan became the bad guy

But how come you missed the point?

No one ever questions you.

Which is why you need me,
Krishna.

10.

Sometimes
The weight of the city
Is too much.

The buildings close in
On one another
Like bodies pressed together
Tightly
In a swaying Mumbai local

Except
There are no stations
No one ever gets out
The crowd never lessens
The bodies stay pressed
Together,
Sweaty
Dirty
Grimy,

Peering into each others'
Most private orifices
Nothing hidden
Nothing private
Nothing sacred.

And then
There are the people
And the cars
And the smoke.

Oh Krishna
Don't even get me started
On the smoke.

Yesterday
I saw the most beautiful
Sliver of the moon
In the early night sky
And it looked yellow
Like it was sickening
With jaundice

They say it is
A sign of a sick liver.

In the many millennia
That you are playing your games

In
This is just another cosmic trick
That you pulled off.

Someone who plays
Is called a player
Someone who lives
Is called a liver.

And we didn't even notice.

We kept thinking the moon's liver
Was jaundiced
When all the time it was the
Liver's soul that was.

Good one,
Krishna.

I don't want to be a sick
Liver,
Krishna.

I'm packing my bags
And heading to the mountains

Only for the weekend
Mind you.

I know I can't escape the game
But even you won't mind
If I take just a little break

And since you are the
Ruler of the Universe
And all that
You think you could
Send me a beautiful moon
On the top of that mountain?

Oh wait
That's not your job
Is it

That's the job of the liver.

Good one again,
Krishna.

11.

I was washing clothes
The other day.

After wandering aimlessly
Through the many rooms
Of the place I call home
Collecting carelessly cast off
Skins of days spent
Working
Playing
Sleeping
Loving
Then sorting them into
Coloureds and Whites
I loaded the machine
Poured in the clean-smelling
Antiseptic
Detergent
And pushed a button.

That's it.

I was washing clothes
The other day

And I remembered other washing days

When I used to be sitting
In the playful waters of our river

And you'd be hanging out
Playing your tireless flute
Weaving your tireless magic.

The magic is gone,
Krishna...

Spin.
Wash.
Dry.

12.

I steal up to the roof
Of this low
Humble house.

All is still around me.

The rickety ladder propped up
Against the rough walls
I scale up
Every morning
Is worn smooth now
By my incessant scampering
Up and down.

The neighbours have been telling us
For years
To build stairs.

I've simply ignored them.

There's something about the ladder
And I feel that building the stairs
Will be something of a treachery.

You know how I am about loyalty.
You've known now for a few millennia.

So the ladder remains
And my feet find their way
Swiftly
Surely
Up its much loved contours.

I'm in a hurry.

The sky is just beginning to
Turn from an inky black
To a watery black

And just as I reach the edge
Of my cement universe

It happens.

The first orange
Pink
Gold
Rays
Pierce through the darkness

And for just one cosmic
Moment
The low flat roofs around me
Are blessed with a touch of magic.

There is no dust
No tired
Dreary washing
Hanging on old
Weary lines
No plastic
No litter
No open sewers.

For just one moment
Everything is
Pure gold.

What an effort you take
To make the beginning
Of my every day
Beautiful.

Good morning,
Krishna

You have a wonderful day too!

13.

I hear you've been
Asking your mother
Why you are
Dark-skinned
And I am
Fair and Lovely.

Stop that,
Krishna!

Your complaints
Are feeding
An entire
Cosmetics
Advertising
Industry
Nexus.

When you are
Lord God
Supreme Being
You've got to be
Careful
What you say.

Poor you,
Krishna.

14.

How does it matter
That you are dark-skinned?

Why should it matter
That I am fair?

It's just a matter
Of a few pigments.

For a fellow
Who is all-knowing
And so wise
It's amazing
How you mind
All this stuff

That simply
Doesn't matter...

Oh how I love you,
Krishna.

15.

Loved.
Lost.
So what?

16.

You are dark,
Krishna.

Dark like the complete
Darkness that I like
To sleep in.

I don't like even a
Little glimmer of light
Penetrating that
Thick
Black
Veil
Of night
That settles around my shoulders
Moulds itself around my sleeping form
And holds me inside it.

Removed
Separate
Far away from the rest of the world.

That's how I like to sleep.

Cocooned in impenetrable dark.

You are dark,
Krishna!

17.

I could sit doing this all day.

This talking to you
And thinking of you
And dreaming with you
Or dreaming of being with you.

But there is a pressure cooker
That I can see from here
And it sits there forlorn
With its lid half open
Its whistle not quite on

It has the stains of yesterday's
Dal and rice
Trailing down its stainless steel
Exterior

And that bothers me.

To put a stain on that which
Can be stainless
Is forgivable
But to leave it there
Isn't.

I could sit here
Like this
Forever

But the stains from the cooker
Have to go

That which is made of
Stainless material
Must shine.

We all have our own
Kurukshetras

No, Krishna?

18.

Why have I always been portrayed
As the jealous one?

You think those stupid
Gopis
With their inane giggling
And their obvious bodies
And their pallus slipping
Oh so innocently
And their wide eyed adoration
Of you
You think I would be jealous of them?

They don't know a thing
About the madness of your music.

They think it's a tune
That escapes your ruby lips

They dance mindlessly
They think…

Oh Krishna,
Do they think at all!

I don't think so!

They are
Stupid
Stupid
Stupid

Why would I be jealous of them?

Oh Krishna,
Why do you smile at them so…

19.

Oh
My
God.

I am the one to blame

I did it

Mea culpa

I am the one
Responsible
For the drivel that is dished out
In the name of prime time television

And you are partly to blame too
Krishna
With a capital K.

You and I together
And our endless story

That has had an unbroken run
Through millennia

We are the inspiration

We are the original
K serial.

Oh
My
God!

20.

Met a child today

Or at least
I saw him
And he saw me

From two sides
Of a glass window.

Strange things they are
These glass windows

They are the dividing lines
Between worlds

You can look across them
At one another

But you rarely
If ever
Cross over.

So he looked at me
And saw a woman
With tightly bunched shoulders
Gripping the steering wheel of
A swanky car
Staring straight ahead
Into the mirage
Of a future
Created by the belched out
Black fumes
Of a pack of metal
At a traffic signal

And I turned my stiff neck
For just a moment
And saw
A tattered boy
With grinning eyes
Trying to sell me a newspaper
Offering me a smile
Complimentary.

For just one moment before
The red turned to green

The woman inside
Smiled back
At the boy outside.

I wonder
What your next disguise
Is going to be,
Krishna.

21.

I just can't stand
Milk.

It isn't so much the milk
Actually

It is more the thick
Cream
That floats up to the surface
And congeals there.

I can't bear it.

To look at it makes the
Bile rise up into my throat

And yet
I plunge my hands into

Cauldron after cauldron
Of cold milk

I pick out the cream
The soft cream that
Lacerates my bile ducts

I pile up that cream
Into one yellow heap

And then I get
My own little revenge
When I churn it into
Leaving its corporeal shape
And becoming butter.

Then I just heat more milk.
To get more cream.

That's how much
I love you,
Krishna.

22.

You got recorded
In the annals of history.

The eyes that record such things
Saw you

Standing tall and proud
And beautiful
Behind Arjuna

Running his chariot
Running the war.

They were not wrong
Those eyes.

They could've sworn it was
You

And you alone
Standing there.

I wasn't there
They swore.
You were all alone.

Ants
I hear
Can only perceive
Two dimensions.

23.

Krishna,
How do you
Manage the entire Universe?

Sometimes it is
Impossible
For me to simply get out of bed

It is at times like these
That I appreciate you the most

No holidays
No time off
No excuses
No later
No let's see
No whatever.

What is it like to be you,
Krishna?

Does being God
Ever get boring?

24.

Boredom
Is the worst.

All evil sprouts
From it.

Not from madness
Or malice
Or some dark
Primordial stuff

But from simple
Innocuous
Boredom.

I think the morons
Who flew their aircraft
Into the twin towers

Were at some remote
Time in their personal
Histories
Very bored young men.

Bored minds
Are like uranium.

Hard
Dense
Malleable
Radio-active.

Make them light up the world,
Krishna.

If you don't
They'll blow it up.

I am so bored
Today.

25.

I get to see myself
In films
And in paintings

And I always laugh.

I look nothing like that.

I dress nothing like that.

And what happened to me
After I turned 40?

And how did I look
Before I caught your eye,
Krishna?

I was a child once

And my waist to hip ratio
Can sometimes be a joke

And I have bad hair days

My jewellery is not always coordinated

My belly isn't always flat.

I'm not a simpering
Song-singing dimwit.

I see myself in films
And in paintings

And I don't see myself at all.

26.

I get so tired
Of the clichés.

Has anyone bothered to
Ask the lotus
How it feels
To be mired in filth?

Who knows if those
Luscious pink petals
Are indeed happy
To have blossomed
In a bog
Or if they are engorged
With loathing
Like a pus-filled boil.

Oh ok

Maybe they are happy,
Krishna.

Must you always be so
Positive
And sunshiney?

Don't you ever want to take
A lotus and shake it
Till it stops being so
Bloody heroic?

Sure it's great to
Cock a snook at the dirt
And bloom like the lotus

But sometimes
Just sometimes
Don't you want to
Throw a tantrum,
Krishna?

I do.

27.

A tantrum about what
You ask me?

Oh just you hear out my list

Oh Krishna,
You are so right

Everything is as it should be
Everything always is

I just forget that
Every once in a while

Thank God I have you…

All these millennia
And I still haven't figured out
How to say
Thank you.

28.

There were peacocks
Woven by loving hands
In gold and silver
And purple and green.

Yard after yard
Of silk
Slipped through
My fingers.

It was like
Someone
Took all the colours
In your kingdom
And poured them
Like a madman
Into yard after yard
Of silk.

There were flimsy
Gauzy
Chiffons
That felt like
Summer breeze
On the skin

There was the
Humble majesty
Of cotton
The seductive
Sensuous
Warp and weft
Of what it means to
Feel like a woman

An endless
Seamless
Celebration
It was

Of all the women I am.

That endless saree
That you gifted Draupadi
Lives on,
Krishna.

We go buy that saree
From crowded bazaars
And fall in love with you
Every time a salesman
Shows us six yards
Of your blessing.

I was out shopping for sarees
Today,
Krishna.

There were peacocks in gold and silver.

29.

I don't often look into the mirror
But today is different

Today I have tied my saree just a little lower
Than I usually do
The smooth curve
Of my fair waist
Is like a smile
An invitation

My dark heavy hair
Is coiled at the nape
Of what the mirror tells me
Is a long neck

My dark eyes
Are even darker today
With the kohl

I have so lovingly applied

There is vermillion
On my forehead
There is a glow
On my cheeks

My slim wrists
Wear bangles today
Silver bells circle
My slim ankles

Tomorrow
I'll go back to my
Jeans and T-shirt

But today
Just for today
I'm going to drive
You crazy,
Krishna.

30.

Look at me,
Krishna

And then look away

I dare you.

31.

There are those times
When I can't reach you

It's like my soul
Is a mansion
From some nightmarish
Fairy tale

Room after monstrous
Room
One door leading
To another
Endless passages
Menacingly glimmering
Lights
Flickering scary shadows
On old
Old walls

Attics
Basements
Cellars
Terraces
A never-ending
Labyrinth
That closes in on me

I run
Like a woman
Possessed
From one horror
To another
Fleeing from myself
And only going
Deeper
And deeper
Into my own self.

I cry out for you,
Krishna.
I search for you,
Krishna.
I cravenly turn out
Stuffed drawers
I look under beds
I rifle through old papers

I rampage through
Entire rooms
Growing more desperate
With every Absence
That I encounter.

It is at times like these
That I know real fear
When I am screaming your name out
Loudly
And all I can hear
Is the sound of my own terror.

Where do you go sometimes,
Krishna?
Leaving me abandoned
Inside my own soul.

32.

And then suddenly
I find you.

In the quiet moment
Between two breaths
I hear you.

In the subtle instant
Between two heartbeats
I live you.

The Absence
Which was a real
Living
Pulsating
Demon
Is vanquished.

You return
From wherever it is
That you choose
To gallivant to

And in your
Presence
I am strong
Again.

Do you ever almost die like this,
Krishna?

33.

I cannot afford
To fear like this.

I cannot afford
To disintegrate

To crumble
Like a dry biscuit

Just because you
Have other stuff
You choose to do

Other than hang around
Being the adhesive
Of my Self
That is.

I am going to be my own
Binding material

I am going to be free of
You.

Great idea

Except

I'd simply die of boredom,
Krishna.

34.

I often catch myself
Stopping in the middle
Of my incessant rushing about

You know how I am
I am always rushing about

There's always something to do

How often have you smiled
That inscrutable smile of yours
And said to me
Rest awhile
Radha

There is this way
In which you say
Radha

That takes my breath away

So I find myself stopping
Ever so often
In my mad tracks

Breaking off in mid sentence

Turning away from an important
Task

It feels like I have something
Infernally urgent
To say to you

And ever so often
I only have to say

Krishna.

35.

Ifeel like such an impostor

Standing up in front
Of the whole world
And leading the life of
A teacher
A housewife
A soldier
A painter
A labourer
A scientist
A socialite
A label
A relationship
A peg
A cog
A fit

When all the time
All through Time
I have only
And always
Been
Radha.

Why must you punish me so,
Krishna?

What a sentence this is.

Sentenced to eternal normalcy.

36.

Went out to lunch with the girls today

Laughed about nothing
Bitched about the slim woman
At the next table
Gave sage advice to one of the girls
Who was having very very serious
Maid trouble
Told her to hold on to the maid
The need for a husband comes and goes
The need for a maid lasts forever
Ate two ice creams
After a huge main course
Two ice creams each
Complained about our
Non-existent
Waistlines

Promised to meet once a week
To jog
Laughed some more
And went our separate ways.

You are not always the centre of my
Universe,
Krishna.

37.

Such a lie
That was

38.

Ever tried travelling
By bus
In the city,
Krishna?

You should

It's quite an experience.

First you have to wait
At a designated place
With no roof
No barriers
No seats
No sense

As you wait
You have to be
Stared at

Whispered about
Brushed against
Whistled at

Then the Sun
Gets into the equation

So you sweat
Frown
And begin to despair

Then there is the wait
Interminable

As bus after bus
Lumbers across
An ugly urban horizon
And imperiously
Lumbers on
Without giving you
So much as a sideways glance
As if it were a spit-spattered Maharaja
And you were a lowly maid servant

Finally a bus deigns to stop
And you jostle your way inside

Where again the karmic cycle
Is repeated

You are
Stared at
Whispered about
Brushed against
Whistled at.

Have you tried travelling by bus,
 Krishna?

You must

If only to see the Radha in every woman
Molested by the filth
In dirty eyes

It's just that she doesn't make
Such a song and dance about it.

Unlike a certain Draupadi.

39.

Sometimes I can't find me.

There are alien voices in my
Head
Voices of reason
Voices of treason

They speak in tones
Of authority

Like they were wearing khaki
And sporting large bossy
Moustaches

They speak in foreign nuances
I know the words
I just can't understand them

They feel like they were there
To bury me

Under layers of bombast
And bravado

And their brand of sense.

I hate those voices in my head,
Krishna.

Stentorian
Stolid
Stodgy
Like congealed cereal.

Which is why I eat breakfast like I do.

Cornflakes with cold milk.

Crisp
Crunchy
Crackling with energy.

You are what you eat

Which makes you
Butter,
Krishna.

40.

Iremember being light once

Every eye on me
As I set the dance floor on fire

My feet rarely if ever touched the ground
My heart defied gravity
I moved like Muhammed Ali
And he moved like a butterfly
Actually the Ali moved like I moved
Past
Present
Future
Get all mixed up
When you are so light

Light hearted
Light footed
Light headed

And then I came crashing down
To the dust
Gravity won
I lost

I remember being light once

Two hours ago

Time
Is your biggest joke,
Krishna.

41.

And let's not even talk
About
Space.

You've had the poor guys
Scratching their venerable
Heads
Over it
Forever.

Is it a thing
Is it a relationship between things
Is it an idea
Can it be measured by a ruler?

There are those who say it can't
But they don't know you,
Do they?

You and your jokes.

Sure it can be measured
But not by a ruler
Poor things
They've got at least that much right

It can be measured
By the Ruler.

Give them the answer,
Krishna.

Sometimes I think you are just one big tomcat
Playing with the mice
Enjoying the game.

Some Ruler you are.

42.

I don't really dislike
Draupadi.

In fact
I positively Love her

I love her fire
Her wit
Her intelligence
Her grace
Her poise
Her courage
Her audacity
Her temerity
Her contempt
Her generosity
Her passion
Her love
Her hatred

She is so alive
She makes me want to sing.

She and I should catch up
Some time.

I'll teach her a thing or two
About how not to become collateral

She'll teach me how to make you go
Saree shopping,
Krishna.

43.

Watering the plants
With gentleness in my heart

Rolling out the dough
With a song in my wrists

Tying ribbons in my younger sister's hair
With love in my fingers

Driving the car
With peace in my shoulders

Walking to work
With joy in my feet.

Loving you
Is such an anatomical exercise,
Krishna.

44.

Sometimes I need to write
Pages

Sometimes all I need to write is
Krishna

45.

It's so difficult
Nowadays
To write like
I used to

Like the sweet waters
Of the swiftly flowing
Yamuna

Clean
Clear
Unsullied

Sparkling brightly
In answer to
The kisses of the Sun

Twinkling
Gurgling

Dancing around
The smooth pebbles
In her path

Swelling tempestuously
In the monsoons

Subsiding
Quietly
After the tantrum
Had passed

Flowing beautifully
Like the blood
Of a fellow with
Perfect cholesterol

It's so difficult
To write like that,
Krishna.

The Yamuna
Is clogged
With the debris
Of civilisation.

46.

Was watching from
My tiny balcony yesterday

As children in the colony
Played hide and seek.

They were so totally immersed
In the game

Joyously they found
Newer and better
Places to hide in

The Seeker
Sought
And never so
In vain.

One child was particularly
Good at hiding

She wore drab clothes
That blended into the
Dull cement
Like a parrot blends into the trees

But she too couldn't hide forever

The Seeker always found
Everything she was looking for.

Eventually.

And I saw both the
Hidden
As well as the
Seeker.

What a game
You have invented,
Krishna.

Pure
Genius.

47.

Pedestrian.

That's how I am
Some times

And I like that

There are times to float
In the
Cold
Pristine
Stratospheric
Clarity
Of Thought

There are times to submerge Oneself
In the dust
The dross

The meanness
Of Being.

You taught me,
Krishna
To dance around trees

I fell right in love
With the
Pedestrian
Then.

Some times
I think
I enjoy it
So much more
Than the
Loftiness
Of restrained
Wisdom.

48.

They say
Dancing around trees
As if it were a bad thing.

I feel so sad for them

Don't you,
Krishna?

The trees
The dance
You
I
What else is there,
Really?

49.

Then there is the
Worship
Of turning up on time
Delivering what you have
Committed
Disciplining your thoughts
Training your body
Respecting your work
Honouring your word
Burning the midnight oil
Keeping on keeping on
Going the distance
Walking the talk

Even when
And especially when
All you want
To do is
Dance.

You are not an
Easy God
To
Worship

Are you,
Krishna?

50.

Just when you
    Permeate me
With your
Presence

You make my
Phone
Ping

I've got you
And
I've got mail

The choices you make me make,
Krishna.

Love
And
Duty.

But I've not spent
All these millennia
With you
Without learning
A few tricks
Of my own.

I open my mail
And reply to
You,
Krishna.

51.

I never go to the temples
They've built to you and I,
Krishna.

It feels strange to see us
Frozen in Time
When in reality
We flow through It
In our eternal dance.

I always listen to the songs
They've written about you and I,
Krishna.

New words
New music
Same dance.

52.

Did you sleep together
They ask

Now how do I answer them,
Krishna?

How do I tell them
That far from sleeping

We wake together
We breathe together
We Be together.

Was it physical between you guys
They ask

Now how do I answer them,
Krishna?

How do I tell them
That there is no was
There is only an eternal
Unbroken
Complete
Is.

My heart bleeds for them,
Krishna.

They don't even know the right questions to ask.

53.

For millennia
Now
People have been
Taking our name
In one unbroken breath

There is no space
Between the two
Utterances
No little crevice
That separates
The enunciation

Radha
and
Krishna

Have long
Long

Long
Ago
Become
RadhaKrishna

The biggest miracles
Are simple

They consist of an
And
That is there one moment
And gone the next

Gone
Forever

54.

In all the many
Lives
That I have lived

My eyes have always been
Black

The fiercest
Darkest
Deepest
Black.

I believe
That's because
No matter what I look at
I only see your

Beautiful
Deep
Dark
Face,

Krishna.

55.

I remember one time
I was old
Very very old

My cheeks were
Wrinkled brown hollows
Sinking without hope
Into a shrivelled toothless cavity

My limbs were frail
Tired
Crisscrossed with the
Stories
Of the many many years
I had lived

My once lustrous hair
Was a wisp of smoke

I was a wisp of smoke

No one would have given me
So much as a passing glance

Who glances at smoke
That is fading away
Into the ether

And I expected no better.

But then a young man came

He was a traveller they said

He walked into my corner
Looked into my black eyes
Held my skeletal hand
And told me
I was the most beautiful
Woman he had ever seen.

There are times you help me live,
Krishna
And times you help me die.

56.

When I was a little girl
My mother told me I was
Beautiful
My brothers thought I was
A pain
My father told me I was his
Princess

My neighbours told them
They were spoiling me
They said I'd never be able
To adjust
To the real world
Where I would be treated
Like just another ordinary
Creature

And then you came along,
Krishna.

Proof if any was needed
That where there is love
There always will be more.

When will they ever learn
That the only way to spoil
A little girl
Is by not bringing her up in love?

57.

He doesn't love you
Anywhere near as much
As you love him

My angry friends tell me
Over and over again.

Most of the times I merely
Smile

But yesterday I gave in
And asked why they say so.

You go around talking about him
Writing songs for him
To him
About him

We've yet to hear one song
He has written for you

So many Hindi films
And not one song
From him
To you.

Now I've got to find a way
To not let them find out
Ever
That I just can't help
Being way more talented than
You are,
Krishna.

58.

I've met many false
Krishnas.

They came in many shapes
In all sizes
And colours

Some loved me falsely
Some led me falsely
Some taught me falsely
Some sought me falsely

They were all different,
Krishna

But ultimately
They were all the same.

They looked like you
They talked like you
In the brightest light of day
They would have passed for you

Until that is
Someone looked at their feet
And saw that they were
Made of clay.

I've met many false Krishnas,
Krishna.

My nightmares are made of clay.

59.

It's a theatre of the
Absurd
An adulation of the
Grotesque

Pull down that which is
Meaningful
Only because it cannot be
Understood
By the anonymous many
Who will not make the effort to
Understand
Not because they can't
But because they simply don't care enough.

That's what it is,
Krishna.

The celebration of mindlessness
By those on soul opiates
For countless others
Who share only numbness in common

Some days the world is
Like
Prime time Television.

60.

You were a cowherd once,
Krishna.

You played your best music
To
And for
Those benign
Bovine
Ears

The cows were your
Audience
The trees and the wind
They were your
Fellow musicians
Oh of course there was always the
Odd adoring Gopi

But you breathed
Divinity
Upon four-legged
Cud-chewing
Herds.

That's when I loved you
Best,
Krishna.

When the music was bigger
Than Krishna

And Krishna closed his eyes
In surrender.

61.

In everyone's imagination
There is a perfect
Love story

And it is called

RadhaKrishna

62.

People imagine us
As being
Lovers
Friends
Partners
Soul mates.

They imagine us
Having
Petty quarrels

They imagine us
Making up

They imagine us
Being the poster couple
Of happily ever after,
Krishna.

They mostly imagine us
Looking drop-dead gorgeous
And singing
And dancing.

They imagine us
Divine
Blessed
Blessing
One.

I wonder if reality
Shapes imagination
Or if it is their imagination
That has shaped our eternal
Reality.

63.

Then there was the day you died,
Krishna.

It was that time when you were
A common soldier.

They draped you in a flag
Bright red it was
I remember

They draped you in that flag
Like so many other
Common soldiers
Slain in battle that day

And consigned you
To the greedy flames
That scorched the night sky
Rising exultantly higher

With every new body
That fuelled their
Insatiable appetite

They fed on my grief
That day
Those monstrous flames

The smoke from that night
Stayed in my eyes
For the rest of my life

It has stayed with me
For the rest of my many
Subsequent lives.

There are many things
I can endure,
Krishna

But I cannot endure
Cigarettes.

64.

One day
I'd like to roam
The streets
At night

Alone
Except for your
Endless Presence.

I see your face
In the first rays
Of the morning sun

But I know you,
Krishna.

I know that you
Really come alive
In the velvety

Black
Of the night sky

I want to feel
That velvet
Against my skin,
Krishna

I want to envelop
My Self in it
I want the stars
To be my diamonds
I want the moon
To sparkle
On my forehead

I want to walk the
Night
Alone,
Krishna

But...
I'm just a woman.

#Radha #Nirbhaya

65.

Have you ever
Felt
Like just running away
From it all?

From the noises
And the voices
And the clamour
And the crowds

And known that you
Can't.

How do you cope
With
The fact of
Impossibility,
Krishna?

With feeling
Sometimes
That you'd
Like to perform
A simple Ctrl Z
That you'd
Want to turn back the
Hands of Time
That you'd
Give anything to just go back

And knowing that you
Can't?

But that is my solace,
Krishna.

If Lord God
Must live
With the apostrophied
Four letter word

Maybe I too can

Live with my own
Can't.

66.

Who has the time
   For us,
Krishna?

They join their hands
In front of
A pretty picture
Once a day

And other than that
They pretty much
Forget that we exist

Except for the odd
And sometimes
Very odd
Filmi paean
To your many games
In which they extol

A fiction
A stereotype
And oftentimes an
Absolute falsehood

Except for that
Who has the time
For us,
Krishna?

Who indeed
Other than
The forgotten
Forsworn
Forlorn
Widows of Vrindavan.

They have the time

Probably because
They have nothing else

No life
No love
No hope
No cheer

Devotion
Sometimes
Is a tonsured head
That everyone can see
And a heart full of hidden
Love
That nobody can.

67.

The city I live in has hills.

They rise in brown and green
Defiance
In the middle of grey concrete.

A couple of times a year
They burst into yellow
And lavender flowers.

They are my saviours
Those hills.

I climb up
Clamber up
Crawl up
Their ancient sides

Depending on the
Strength in my
Soul

And once I reach
Their ancient
Weathered
Crumbly tops
I always pause
And take a deep
Deep
Breath.

There is something
Reassuring
About the smell of the old
Soil.

It smells like
Home,
Krishna.

It feels like
You and I.

68.

How can you not like
Milk
And cream

They taunt me

Your Krishna loves it so
They jeer.

We are One
I answer

But we are not the same.

He loves milk
I love poetry

He makes the music
I make the dance

Our whole is greater
Than the addition of our similarities
And the subtraction of our differences

That's why I don't like
Milk and cream

Because it is important
That I don't

Because we are different
Because we are One

Because we are RadhaKrishna.

Not Narcissus.

69.

I always associate
The rains
With your birth

With your mother
Swaddling you in love
Your father carrying you
On his head
In a wicker basket
And walking through
A swollen
Flooded
River.

The waters parted
For your father
They say

Actually
They parted for you
Didn't they,
Krishna?

You were a miracle
From the moment
Of your birth

And the rains
Remind me of that
Moment

I associate the
Rains
With miracles,
Krishna.

How very agrarian of me.

70.

Play a sweet melody
 Tonight,
Krishna.

Let your flute
Soothe my soul.

I have laid down my weapons
I have taken off my armour
The battle will commence
Once more at the light of day

But the fight has gone out of today
The light has gone out of today

Play a sweet
Sweet

Melody,
Krishna.
My soul is weary tonight
And tomorrow is only
A dark night away.

71.

Romance makes me
Sigh.

In paperback
On silver screen
It makes me sigh.

He looks at her
She looks back at him

The blood rushes to his
Head
And other parts of his anatomy
Of course
But we don't talk about such
Things
In the romances that I sigh over

So the blood rushes to his head
And a delicious shiver runs down her spine

And slowly
In a delicate movement
They fall into one another

Sometimes there is the delirium
Of a new-found passion
Sometimes there is the gentle awakening
Of a dormant desire

Sometimes there is the quick
Sharp intake of breath
Sometimes there is the moan
That barely escapes parted lips

Pulses quicken
Time slows down
Nothing seems to matter
Other than the moment
And the romance,

In all these millennia,
Krishna
You've never sent me roses.

72.

Just saying

That you could be
Lord God
And Master of the Universe

But even you don't have
All the answers

All these millennia
Of serenading her
With divine music

And she says you've never sent her roses

Don't you just love the
Way
I can still make your jaw drop,
Krishna?

73.

When you walked into that
Store
And told the beaten down woman
That she had magic in her fingers
That she should stop trying to peddle
Stationery
And invest herself in painting all the
Stuff she could lay her hands on

When you picked out her incredible
Talent from the idle scribbles on her
Notepad
And made it come alive in front of her eyes

When you went and bought her first
Hand-painted coffee mug
And sent friends along to place orders
For their own

You didn't just give her a business idea

You don't fool me for a moment,
Krishna.

You have to rush around saving the
World
From serious bad guys
With evil designs

And you still find it important
To stop
And show a person
The possibility of divine
Personal
Magic.

Don't tell me you gave that woman
A business idea.

You saved her soul.

You gave her
Joy
Beauty
Grace
Fulfillment

And that's why I love you,
Krishna.

Because of a woman
Who smiles
When she paints pink flowers
On a mug.

74.

I went to the bazaars
Of Benaras
On a quest
That took me through
Narrow
Dizzyingly narrow lanes
Across the mingled
Heady stench
Of lives lived
In irreverent intimacy

No respect
For ideas
Like privacy
And personal
And space

When you go to the
Bazaars of Benaras

You inhale all of
Benaras in one breath

Past
Present
Death
Life
Beauty
Beast
Benaras is the place
Where contradictions
Not only coexist
In peace
They thrive
They flourish
Like fungus
On old bread.

And that is where
My quest took me

In search of hands
That would weave me
Benediction.

Weaver after weaver
I met

And to
Weaver after weaver
I made my particular request

Purple
Green
Brown
Turquoise
Yellow
Iridescent
Jewel-bright colours.
They should ripple
With a life of their own.

They all looked at me like
I was a little mad,
Krishna.

And maybe I was
Maybe I am

But then at last
I found him
An old man
Nearly blind

But my words
Lit a light
In those milky cataracts
His toothless mouth
Cracked open into a wide grin
The skin on his face
Visibly breaking
Like it hadn't been employed
For smiling
In too long.

He heard my strange
Request
For a saree that danced

He turned his head away
From me
Barely concealing his
Divine joy
He ran his hands
Lovingly
Across his old
Disused
Loom

And muttered

You want me to weave
You a peacock feather

You must be
Radha.

75.

They came to me
And said
I was lazy,
Krishna.

That I should write
Prose
In detail
A thousand pages
A million words

That the
Story of
RadhaKrishna
Should be
A big
Fat
Volume.

I simply smiled
And told them
It was.

And maybe
It was they
Who were lazy

Counting the words
And not uncovering the
Fat
Voluminous
World of meaning
Sublimated in each.

The story of
RadhaKrishna
Lies not so much
In the writing
As in the reading
Not so much in the reading
As in the feeling.

Poetry
Needs to be felt

They don't teach that
In schools,
Krishna.

Maybe in your next
Avatar
You should be
Minister for Education.

76.

Classic good looks.

Now I don't know
What that means.

From long neck
To tiny feet
To wide hips
To thick lips
To peaches and roses
To almond eyes
To straight hair
To curly hair
To pointy nose
To small ears

It could mean
Anything

Depends on
Who is looking.

But when I see
Some of the statues
They've built
Of you and I,
Krishna
I must admit
That the people
Who were doing
The looking

Had classic good looks.

77.

Our chroniclers
Got some things right
And completely missed out
On some.

They got the flute
And the Gopis
And the cows
And the dancing
And the flirting
And the teasing
And the way that
Every parting
Felt like a little
Death.

They got all that
Right.

But they didn't stop
And ask us
What we did in all those
Long eras
When we were not
Busy
Running around trees
When you were not
Busy
Saving the world
When I was not
Busy
Being jealous of your
Many many distractions.

If they had
They would've known
The little things.

How I love mangoes
And you are a cat person

How we like to solve
Crossword puzzles
With pencils that are never
Very sharp

How you drink your tea

With lots of sugar
And no milk

Which totally goes against
The Image

How I have always had a dog
And although I love you,
Krishna
There is that special corner
Of my Being
That is reserved parking
For a woman's best friend

And how I hate
That
Far too many people
Will think
Diamond
And not
Dog
When they read that.

They don't know
Because they didn't ask
That we sleep with our backs
Touching

It's like we are connected
From the base of our
Spines.

They chronicled us
Grinning into
The camera,
Krishna

But they didn't
Really
Get the picture.

78.

Brave
Kind
Loyal
Shrewd
Forgiving
Unforgiving
Wise
Child-like
Gracious
Ungracious
Funny
Grave
Naughty
Nice

For a God
You are remarkably
Human,
Krishna.

You are a remarkable
Proof
That humans are capable
Of
Divine Creation.

79.

The little girl
Was playing
In her world of
Make
Believe.

There was a beautiful
Mountain
And a river that danced
And smooth
Round
Pebbles
In the colours of the
Rainbow.

She sat with
Her feet immersed
In the cool
Waters

Of the swift-flowing
River
Humming a happy song
Gazing up
At a blue
Blue sky
With her clear
Black
Black eyes

As she sat in
Her shanty
Surrounded
By the stench
Of her dead drunk
Father
In the redolent
Squalor
Of a 6 by 6
Tarpaulin covered
Shack
The little girl
Felt the cool
Water
On her grubby feet.

That's how she
Made it

That's how she survived

Because you gave her
The gift
Of
Make
Believe,
Krishna.

80.

You can do
Just
About
Anything

You think
You could
Get rid
Of my
Double chin,
Krishna?

Or are you just
Going to give
Me your standard
God helps those
Who go to the gym
Spiel?

All that spectacular
Sunrise
And dewdrops
On roses
All that is the
Easy magic

Getting rid
Of my double chin
Overnight

Now that would
Fall in the class
Of major miracle

You think you could
Pull it off,
Krishna?

You can do
Just
About
Anything.

81.

My best songs
To you,
Krishna
Are the ones
For whom
I could never
Find the words.

82.

I like letting the feeling
Linger
In my soul

Like the aftertaste
Of cardammom

Like the scent of a woman
Long after she has walked out of a room

I like that
Living memory

I like the power
To prolong reality

To stretch a moment
Like it were made of
Elastic

To keep a moment
Alive
After it has passed

To keep it alive
Through eternity.

That's why I write
Poetry,
Krishna.

I like playing
Mind games
With
Reality.

83.

Poetry is a conjuror's trick.

It captures the
Essence of
What once was
Summons it out of nowhere
And keeps it
Suspended
Like the conjuror's sleeping woman
On swords.

Soon the conjuror
Takes away the swords
That support the
Suspended
Supine
Woman

And we gasp
In wonder
As the sequinned
Woman
Slumbers
In thin air.

Poetry is like that

Capturing a sequinned moment
In words and pauses and rhythm and metre

And holding that moment aloft
Unsupported
Magical
In front of awestruck eyes.

It is all an illusion

Which is what makes it so real.

You are the master conjuror,
Krishna.

You are the master poet

And we are your sequinned women
We are the admiring audience

We are the words
We are the pauses

Sometimes one.
At other times another.

What an artist you are,
Krishna

What a trickster.

84.

I wonder how
They
Do it,
Krishna.

Hundreds of thousands
Of people
Across I don't even remember
How many
Lifetimes
All blundering about
Bleary eyed
Searching for
Meaning.

What is this
Evil trickery
That you perpetuate,
Krishna?

That they hold
Themselves
In the wholeness
Of Being
And yet the
Meaning
Escapes their outstretched
Souls.

You have immersed me
In the arcane
Made me muddle through
The mundane
You have blessed me with
The ridiculous
You have tortured me with
Stupid

But you have never
Ever
Robbed me of
Meaning,
Krishna.

And for that
I remain
Yours Truly

85.

It's alright,
Krishna.

Arjuna will break
When you most need him to be strong

Yudhdhishtir will succumb
To his good guy image

Bhima
He's probably the best of the lot
He'll always be difficult
But he'll always be himself

The twins will hover
Like unresolved issues
At the edge of the drama

Karna will be
Your biggest failure

Duryodhana will always
Be bewildered by your behaviour

Everyone will always
Expect you to take care of everything.

It's alright,
Krishna

You can always come to me
And take off your smile.

Even Gods need a place
To call Home.

86.

Have you ever felt like
Champagne,
Krishna?

All light
And golden
And bubbling with joy?

Sometimes
On days that feel like
I am made of treacle
Thick
Sweet
Sticky

Sometimes
On days that feel like
I am made of tar
Thick

Black
Sticky

On those days
I pop a cork
Somewhere deep inside
My soul

And slowly
I begin to feel like
I am made of champagne.

You should try it,
Krishna
Not drinking champagne
Being it.

But then again
Maybe there is a reason
Why champagne
Is the God of grape juice

Maybe Champagne
Is just you
In a bottle.

87.

Some days I wear
Working clothes
Other days I wear
Clothes that work

Not that you would
Notice,
Krishna.

You've called me
Beautiful
When I'm looking like
The moon's surface
You've ignored me
When I shone
Like
The moon.

Fashion is wasted
When your
Boyfriend
Is God.

88.

Did I just say
Boyfriend?

Now that's the problem
With you,
Krishna.

There are simply
No labels
That I can paste
On that divine forehead of yours.

Maybe I should invent some

Maybe I should admit
That I've tried
And failed.

I remember your mother telling me
How as a child it was impossible
To keep you in one place
How you slipped through
Her searching fingers
How you always escaped.

I should have learnt
Early,
Krishna

You always escape

Definition.

And maybe I have been looking at
This
All wrong.

Maybe there are labels

There is just not enough
Adhesive
In your Universe
To make them
Stick
To that
Divine forehead of yours.

89.

He sat
With his back firmly turned
To the busyness of civilisation

Thin bony shoulders
Straight as a
General's

A ragged turban
Wrapped
In that unintendedly
Fashionable ease
That those who are born
With style have.

He sat on the earth
That was not nearly
As brown
As the back of his neck

And stared determinedly
Out at the distant horizon
As cars rushed
Past
Him
And one another
On the hot
Black
Smooth
Road
To nowhere.

I only caught a fleeting
Glimpse
Of him

As I too went
Nowhere
At a 100 km an hour.

The thin brown man
And his meagre
Bony
Cows

On a bare brown
Hill slope
At the edge

Of a black
Fast
Lane.

I don't know
Why he stayed in my mind,
Krishna.

But then I do.

I can spot you
From the straightness
Of your shoulders

Even at a 100 kilometers per hour.

90.

They don't know
The real cost
Of war.

There have been many
Estimates
Over the eons

But no one has been
Able to calculate
What the family squabble
Really cost.

You went away
From
Vrindavan

I stayed back

The real cost
Of Kurukshetra

Was the moment
When you disappeared
Over the horizon
At the end of our universe

That moment
When you looked back
And couldn't see me
When I strained my eyes
But couldn't see you

The monumental
Incalculable
Cost
Of war
Was an empty horizon.

It always has been,
Krishna.

91.

Through the ages
They have been
Wondering

Whatever happened
To her
After
Krishna
Left Vrindavan

And every once in a while

I hear an old grandmother
With a twinkle in her eyes
Tell an adoring
Granddaughter

Krishna never left
Radha never stayed back

Wherever they went
They were One

RadhaKrishna fought and won
In Kurukshetra
RadhaKrishna tended cows
Back in Vrindavan.

We owe our lives
To kind
Old
Grandmothers,
Krishna.

92.

Then there are others
Who shout
Angrily

Radha
Never existed

She was just a figment
Of some stupid
Romantics' imagination.

I wonder what makes them so angry

The thought that
A love like
Ours

Is not possible,
Krishna

Or

The more real thought
That it is.

93.

S.

On that day
When you disappeared
Over the horizon
For ever
I went back
To our house
With a heart
That felt like
It would annihilate
Me with
Pure
Pain

And I picked up
The flute

That you had left behind
And broke it.

You should have known
Better,
Krishna
Than to leave behind
An instrument
That was dead
Without
Your breath.

94.

There are many
  Ways
Of
Committing suicide

Some people hang themselves

Some
Break flutes

95.

What a stuck up
Woman

Who does she think she
Is

Princess of Moo?
Queen of Cows?

Her Royal Highness
The Tender of Herds?

Why couldn't she just
Pack her bags
And leave
With her precious
Krishna?

That's what women do
They go where their man goes

Who does she
Think
She is?

They have poured their
Scorn
On me
Century after century

And yet
I haven't answered them.

I should
I think.

And that's the whole point.

I think.

I am.

And I had my destiny

Just like Krishna had his.

Mine was to tend cows

His
To tend other animals.

I surrendered my soul
To
Krishna,
Scornful people

My destiny
Was my very own.

96.

Holding on
Takes strength

Letting go
Takes power

I must have been the
Most
Powerful
Woman
In history,
Krishna...

97.

Everything
Has changed,
Krishna.

That road that you took
Out of Vrindavan
Still exists

But everything about
It has changed.

It is just an ordinary
Dirty by-lane now

Crowded
Filthy
Narrow

Ugly buildings
Have replaced
The beautiful basil hedges

There is smoke
There is noise
There are so many
People,
Krishna

But the horizon
Is still empty.

98.

That moment
When we could
No longer
See
Each other

That moment
Of the
Empty horizon

That was the
Moment of
Magic

We never
Saw
Each other again

And yet
We were
Never
Separate

Ever
Again.

That empty horizon
Moment
Was when the
And
Disappeared

From that moment onwards
We ceased to be
Radha
And
Krishna

We became
RadhaKrishna.

They say alloys are made
In furnaces.

99.

Alloys.

Now that is an
Interesting
Metaphor.

Iron by itself is brittle
And prone to
Rust

Aluminium by itself
Is very light
But much too soft
And far too weak

So some really smart

People

Metallurgists
We call them

Combine these
Metals with other
Stuff
And make them
Stronger
Harder
Lighter
Or
Better in some other way.

But first they put them through
Hell fires,
Krishna.

Tears
Are molten metal.

100.

A firm Hand took
The two metals
And plunged them
Into fire.

The metals cried out
In pure agony.
They begged
They pleaded
They couldn't bear the
Pain.

The Hand was deaf
It paid them no heed.

And slowly the fire
Began to cool.

Something emerged
From the dying embers
Something that glowed
From within

As if the fire
Had become
A part of its soul

Slowly that glowing
Soul
Solidified
Into its new form

And the two metals
Could never be
Separated
Again.

Our story is taught
In chemistry labs,
Krishna.

They always said
We had
Chemistry.

What they didn't
Say
Because they don't
Know
Is that we
Are
Chemistry,
Krishna.

101.

I've spent my whole
Life
Talking to you
But was it just me
Talking to me

You are in my head
My heart
My soul,
Krishna

And I wish you'd stop smiling
That superior smile of yours
Like you knew something I didn't
Like you knew everything
And I didn't.

There
That's better.

There are no boundaries,
Krishna.
There is no you
And no me
Or is it I

The time for grammar
Is long past

There is just this
Moment
And in this moment
We are One.